Unique Love

Quinton Simpson

Unique Love: Quinton Simpson

This book is a work of poetry. Unless otherwise noted, the author and the publisher make no explicit guarantees as to the accuracy of the information contained in this book and in some cases; names of people places have been altered to protect their privacy.

© 2014For Quinton Simpson & Published By Maximize Publishing Inc. & Michael McCain. Bronx New York, All Rights Reserved.

No part of this book may be reproduced, stored in a retrieval system, or transmitted by any means without the written permission of the author.

First Published for:
Maximize Publishing Inc.

ISBN-13:
978-0692240687 (Maximize Publishing Inc.)

ISBN-10:
0692240683

Table Of Contents

Dedication...7

Part I..9

Part II...51

Part III..101

Unique Love: Quinton Simpson

Unique Love

Quinton Simpson

Unique Love: Quinton Simpson

Dedication

I would like to dedicate this book to my mother (Vera Daniels) and my grandmother (Helen Williams) these two women never gave up on me. They always encourage me to keep writing and never give up. My mother was always that push in my life. When others didn't believe in me and said it couldn't be done. My mother told me different and I love her so much. I would also like to thank my grandmother for keeping me in her prayers, for loving me and always told me to keep my head up because God has the last say so. Mother you're that rock in my life, the blood that run through my veins and the smile on my face. Thank you for pushing and loving me more than anything.

Unique Love: Quinton Simpson

Part I

Unique Love: Quinton Simpson

Bleeding Love

My heart is bleeding love

I'm going crazy for you

And the love is very strong

If you cut my heart open

I'll continue to bleed love

For you

I'm ready to see your face

People are trying to pull me

Away from you

But they can't because I'm

Bleeding love for you

Unique Love: Quinton Simpson

Our love is stronger than ever

Every time I close my eyes my heart,

Soul and mind bleed love

You're my everything and more

I can't go a day without you or

Your love

The two of you mean so much

Whenever things seem to go crazy

I think of your love

I know it's going to bring happiness, joy

And peace in my life

I hope your love keep bleeding in my world

Bleeding Love

Almost

Almost doesn't count in my life

I gave you one hundred percent

Of me and you still walked over me

You really hurt me

I couldn't believe you

Almost never counted with me

You hurt me so bad

I gave you my life and you always

Said you almost this and that

That's what I got tired of hearing

That word is dead in my life

Unique Love: Quinton Simpson

I was in love with you and not almost

I really can't believe you

I guess you almost married me

Had my hopes up and thinking

My life was about to change

Almost got the very best of me

I can't stop thinking about it

I'm lost, sad and hurt

I wish you would of almost out

Of my life

I gave you the world, showed love

Like no other and believe in you

I'm not with that almost love

        Almost

All I Want Is You

Baby you're all I want

I don't see no one but you

My heart doesn't want anybody else

You're my heart, soul and you complete me

I can't imagine living in this world with you

You're my best friend and all I want is you

You're my baby

I love all of the special times we shared

Your life meant the world to me

You're my pride and joy

I don't care about the next chick

She can't do it like you can

Unique Love: Quinton Simpson

You're all I think about and more

No one can ever replace you

I love you so much

Your love is so powerful

People can't compare you to others

You always bring out the best in me

And I love you baby

There's nothing in this world

I want but you

You bring love to my life

        All I Want Is You

Unique Love: Quinton Simpson

Always Be My Baby

You'll always be my baby

You're my make it happen

Favorite lady and my world

I love you so much

You'll always be a part of my heart

When things got though in my life

You was their until the end

You kept me grounded, humble and filled with joy

You'll always be my number one baby

You're the light that shine in me

The sparkle in my eye and the smile on my face

Unique Love: Quinton Simpson

You're my boo thang

I'm in love with you

And without you I'm worthless

Always Be My Baby

Anytime

We can have sex anytime and any place

I'm willing to make this happen

Let's make love any time of the day

I'm ready for some sexually healing

You can enter your pretty little lips

Unique Love: Quinton Simpson

Into my mouth anytime of the day

I'm waiting to feel your sexy, soft and amazing lips

Make me feel like a king

Get on top of me and

Ride me any time of the day

Make my toes curl and my body shake

I'm ready for that any time love

I need something that's going to ease my mind

Baby don't be scared to give me

Some of that amazing any time love

                        Any time

Be A Man About It

Man up and tell me the truth

If you don't want me please

Let me know

Don't keep me waiting

I love you, gave you my heart

And have always believed in you

Be a man about the situation

And let me go

You're always lying, cheating

And I'm the best thing you ever had

You said you loved me but I knew better

In my heart I knew it was all a dream

Unique Love: Quinton Simpson

When is the cheating and lying going to stop?

I was your ride or die

Always kept it real

And gave you whatever

Just be a man about it

And tell me the truth

        Be A Man About It

Booty Call

Girl you're just a booty call

I only want you when the sex

Is needed

Unique Love: Quinton Simpson

You don't mean anything to me

Never will I ever respect you

Because you're only what we

Call a b c (booty call) which is always free

I'll never have respect for a woman who's

Only known for a booty call

You mean the world nothing and men

Will always use you

Respect is what you need

I love you because when I'm in need

Of some good sex

You're always their

I don't feel sorry nor care for you

A free booty call like you should get

Tired of laying on your back for free

Unique Love: Quinton Simpson

You make it hard for all of the good women

Whenever men won't some free booty

They call a rat like you

It's free, good and amazing

Learn about life because being a booty call

Isn't going to get you far in life

I would say do better but you are not

Because you were once everybody booty

But now you only answer when you're called

        Booty Call

Broken Hearted

My heart is broken, torn and cracked

The pain is killing me

I gave you my trust and love

You stab my heart

Crushed my world

And drained my mind

I gave you the best I had

Why break a heart that was

Loving, caring and awesome

You was the blood that kept my heart pumping

The voice that always said I love you

And the ear that always listen

I tried to give you the world and all but that didn't work

Because you still broke my heart

Broken Hearted

Can We Talk

Baby can we talk for a minute

I love you, need you

And very much understand you

I'm lonely, hurt, sad

Unique Love: Quinton Simpson

And baby I love you so much

You're my joy and heart

Can we talk this love thing through?

I'm crying, going crazy and want to hurt myself

My feelings is deep, my love is broken

And my soul is lost

You're my world, love and peace

Baby I truly love you and

Can we sit down and talk for a minute

        Can We Talk

Can't Get Enough

I can't get enough of love

It's something about it that

Make my life happy

It always bring out the best in me

And I love it so much

I can't get enough of the feeling

Power and the way it make me feel

Love is powerful, caring and I can't

Get enough of it

Love humble me with joy

My soul is always seeking it

It's real, kind and joyful

Love means a lot to me

Unique Love: Quinton Simpson

I'm happy to be in love but I

Want more

Love free my mind, soul and life

When I think of love my heart think

Of life

It's special than anything I know

And I want more of it

Love please bring more my way

I can't get enough of you

I need all of you and more

Come on baby because I'm

Crazy about you

I can't get enough of you

                Can't Get Enough

Come With Me

Come and enjoy life with me

Let me treat you like the queen you are

I'm willing to love and take care of you

I want to celebrate your life

So you can be with me

Come into my life and make it right

Come with me to another world

So you can enjoy life, my self

And love.

I want to enjoy you

Unique Love: Quinton Simpson

Make me happy baby

And travel this journey with me

I need you and I really love you

So come with me and enjoy life

Come With Me

Deep

I want to feel you deep inside of me

I want every inch of it.

Make that penis hit my private part

Play in it with your tongue.

Tongue me down deep

Make my vagina lips fold.

Unique Love: Quinton Simpson

I need some good deep penis.

Make me cry tears of love.

It's not right unless you're hung from the floor

My legs are open and im waiting to be played in deep.

My vagina lips are throbbing and my mind is horny.

Beat the vagina deep and long.

My mouth is waiting to deep throat that penis

And my anus is ready

Give me some of that good deep loving.

                    Deep

Don't Let Go

Please don't let go of my heart

I love, care and need you

You're my better half

And I can't live without you

In my life

My mind is hungry for your soul and love

I can't let go of you

I can't make it in this world without you

You're my everything

And I need you to stay

I'm in love with your heart

Mind and soul

Unique Love: Quinton Simpson

Please don't let go of me

I'm in love with you

And I need you the most

        Don't Let Go

Don't Forget About Us

Please don't forget about us or our love

We were two diamonds in the rough

Our love was like know other

I gave you my life and you gave me your love

You were my queen and I were your king

You were always my favorite girl

Unique Love: Quinton Simpson

I once called you ma and you called me pa

Love was our favorite friend

We had the relationship others wanted

But couldn't have

I was your secret and you was my garden

We had that killer love

That love that will make your toes crawl

Your eyes roll back and your body shaking

That's what you call real and amazing love

So baby whatever you do

Don't forget about us

Because we had that killer love

        Don't Forget About Us

Unique Love: Quinton Simpson

Don't Take It personal

I don't think we should be together

It's nothing personal

I'm trying to figure things out

You mean a lot to me and you'll

Give me the world but I need to

Find myself

I'll always care for you

You brought joy and love to my life

I can remember when I first meet you

Your smile was so amazing

It touch my heart with love

I knew you would have made a good wife

Unique Love: Quinton Simpson

I wasn't ready for the marriage thing and it's nothing personal

I'm trying to live and work out my life

I know you're always going to be that shoulder

To cry on, that ear who always listen and the

Heart that always love

You really mean a lot to me but I don't

Think we can take it any further

And it's not you

It's me and don't take it personal

You'll always be my best friend, right hand lady

And my number one fan

I knew you wanted this to be a relationship

And more but I wasn't ready

Don't get mad at me baby because you

Unique Love: Quinton Simpson

Was my world

Please don't take this personal

You'll always be the love of my life

Don't Take It Personal

Dreaming Of You

Dreaming of you is like dreaming of water

You're always running through my mind

And flowing through my heart

You were once my wife

And I were your husband

I can't stop dreaming of you

Unique Love: Quinton Simpson

Baby you were my joy, peace and happiness

I can't go a day without dreaming of you

And only you

You're my mind, understanding and my backbone

Dreaming of you is what kept my life together

The most I dream of you

The happier my soul and heart get

You mean the world to me

And that's why I'm forever dreaming of you

                    Dreaming Of You

Unique Love: Quinton Simpson

Every Time I Close My eyes

I hate to close my eyes because I'm

Always thinking of you

And that's something I really hate

You took me through hell and back

You always said you loved me but I

Didn't believe you

Your heart played with me

When it came down to love

I gave you the best that I had

Why treat me like dirt

Unique Love: Quinton Simpson

My heart thought you was the best thing ever

I should've known a lot better

Every time I close my eyes

All I see is darkness and hate

You treat me worse than a

Whore on the street

I was better than that

If I could kill you I would

You only caused me stress

With a lot of pain

Every time I close my eyes I see

Myself putting you away for the good

Like you don't deserve to live

                    Every time I Close My Eyes

Finding My way Back

I'm trying to find my way back in your life

You was my life, peace and my better half

I'm really missing you

I need you back in my life

And would love you back

I'm not giving up

How can I find my way back in your life

You was that kick in my heart, the size of my feet

And the air in my tires

I'm so hoping to find

Unique Love: Quinton Simpson

My way back in your life

You were that love in my eyes

And that shine in my soul

You're my find and your way

So let's find our way back in each other life's

                Finding My Way Back

For You I Will

I'll do anything for you

If you ask me to swim

In the deepest ocean for

You I will

Unique Love: Quinton Simpson

You've been that great one in my life

And I thank you for it

If you ever ask me to run

Around the world and back

I will because you've shown

Me love, respect and gave me joy

I'll do anything just for you

For you I'll climb the highest peak

Run the hardest race and smile throughout

The sun

Baby you're my moon and all

You shine like know other

The glow on your face keeps me

Happy and your eyes are always amazing

Unique Love: Quinton Simpson

For you I'll give my all and more

You're my peace, lover and best friend

So I'll do anything to please you

For you I will love to the max

Because I know you will bring out the best

In me.

    For You I Will

Going Crazy

Girl you have me going crazy over you

Your private part has me whipped

When I get around you

My mind can't think

It's something about you

You have a tight hold on me

Unique Love: Quinton Simpson

Your private part has me

Thinking of you instead of myself

That thing is powerful and amazing

Whenever I'm playing in it

My mind begin to dance in all 50 states

And that's something I can't take

You have that good stuff

It's always fighting my mind

That good good have me going crazy

My body is crazy for your sweet love

Going crazy is what I can't help

It has me glued to you and only you

                    Going Crazy

Unique Love: Quinton Simpson

Hate That I Love You

I hate that I love you

You treated me like nothing

Took me thorough hell and didn't love me

I gave you my heart and more

I stop living my life for you

I didn't see anyone but you

You were my best friend, lover

And my life

I put you above the rest

Because I thought you were the best

Unique Love: Quinton Simpson

I was that ride or die

Put my life on the line

And even went the extra mile for you

I guess it was all a dream

I hate I love you so much

Hate That I Love You

He is

He is the king in my life

The shield that protect my heart

And the sex in my eyes

I love him so much

Unique Love: Quinton Simpson

He is the slang in my walk,

The sound of my voice and the

Shake of my body

He is the love of my life

The man that make things happen

And the shine in my life

I love him more than I love myself

He complete me and he is my

Number one dream

He is the song in my head, the

Hello in my voice and the kiss of my lips

He is my everything and more

He is my little star, my heart and my trust

He means the world to me

He is the ear that listens, the

Unique Love: Quinton Simpson

Heart that trust and the tears that cry

He is my boo boo, my main man

And my soul mate

He is more than just life

He is my man, lover and the one

I'm going to be with forever

He is my everything

        He Is

I Can't

I can't stop loving you

You're my king and lover

Unique Love: Quinton Simpson

You make my world go around

I can't get enough of you

You're sexy, honest and caring

I can't live without you in my life

I can't love the rest

Because you're my best

You held me down when things got tough

Made my life happen and kept it real

I can't sleep without you

You're my bear to hold on too

The sun that melts my heart and the eyes that say I love you

                    I Can't

Part II

Unique Love: Quinton Simpson

Unique Love: Quinton Simpson

I Love Me Some Him

I don't think I'll ever love someone

Else the same

You know you're the best

And you always bring out the best in me

You're the love of my life

I love having you as my king

I really love me some you

You keep me grounded, in

Love and happy

You'll always be the best man ever

And that's why I love me some you

Unique Love: Quinton Simpson

Your eye touches my soul

Your heart ease my pain and

Your love makes everything better

When things are bad you help me

Through and I would like to thank you

Your kindness keep me strong, your

Trust keep me believing and your

Amazing power keep me very happy

I can't seem to love you enough but

I can say now and forever that I love

Me some him and only him

        I Love Me Some Him

I Miss You

I miss your touch, love

And your heart.

You were my baby, joy

And heart.

You meant the world to me.

Without you in my life I can't function nor live.

You was my rock, the love of my life

And my soul

You were my best friend and lover.

My life is lost without you

Im hurting, sad and lost

Unique Love: Quinton Simpson

You mean so much to me

I was always your number one guy and more

I miss you because you were the lung in my life

The laughter on my face and th4e best man I ever had

I Miss You

I Wanna Be Loved

Baby I just wanna be loved

I feel lost without you in my life

I'm tired of the lonely nights

My life need to be love

I need that special you in my world

Unique Love: Quinton Simpson

I wanna take chances with you but

I'm scared

I would love to build a lifetime with you

My heart is telling me one thing and my mind

Isn't ready

I think I'm going to let my heart do the talking

I just wanna be loved

All I've been through and done

I deserve to be love

I'll give you my best and more

I've enjoyed the single life long enough

My weakness has kept me down

I stress more about love

My heart, soul and life just

Wanna be love

Unique Love: Quinton Simpson

I'm not asking for much but I'm

Scared at the same time

I'm thinking love isn't going to treat me well

I'm going to give love a try

      I Wanna Be Loved

I Wanna

I wanna know what turn you on

So I can be your all

Baby what make you sad

So I can make you smile

I love you and I'll do anything

To make you happy

Unique Love: Quinton Simpson

Just let me know because I wanna

Know what make you love

So I can be that and more

I wanna know you and only you

Sit down and talk to me

My heart wanna know the good, bad and ugly about you

I wanna know what make your heart happy

And overwhelm with joy

So I can be that love in your life

I wanna keep a smile on your face

And love in your heart

I never want you to have a dull moment

In your life

So tell me how to cheer you up

I only wanna make you happy

Unique Love: Quinton Simpson

I want to clear your mind

But if you don't tell me

I can't and I really want to know

I wanna

I Wish I Wasn't

I've always wish I wasn't

In love with you

The way you treat me is sad

I've always been there for you

I went without, gave you my last

And you didn't show a thank you

Unique Love: Quinton Simpson

Loving you isn't easy

And I wish I wasn't in love with you

You're my heart but you treat me

Like nothing

You always say you love me

Care and wanted to be with me

I do not believe it

I put my all ion you, did backwards

Flips and even worked my life crazy

Over you

Baby I really love you

But you don't seem to care

This is why I wish I wasn't in

Love with you

        I Wish I Wasn't

Unique Love: Quinton Simpson

I Would

I would love to come in

Your room on a lonely night

And put rose peddles

 all over your bed

I would love to run you a hot

Bubble bath, take off your clothes

And massage your body.

Making you feel like a queen.

I would love to lay you in the bed

Begin licking you from top to bottom

Stopping at your sexy part.

Making your toes curl, your body begin to shake

Unique Love: Quinton Simpson

And your legs gripping my head.

I want your body to flow with me

Confront me and love me.

You are my lady.

I would love for you to ride my face, get my tongue wet

And make my body fold.

I would love to have some of that good wet loving.

    I Would

Unique Love: Quinton Simpson

If I Was Your Man

Baby girl if I was your man

I'll be the best ever

My heart will love, take care of you

And make you my number one

I'll take you on amazing trips, play

And love on your kids

Let me be your man

If I was your man

I'll bring joy, peace

And love to your life

I'm the man you need

And I'll always love you

Let me be that smile in your life

Unique Love: Quinton Simpson

We'll go through the good, bad

And the pretty together

I'll give you the clothes off of my back

The shoes off of my feet and the love

Out of my heart

If I was your man

If I was your man

I'll love to be your husband

The father of your kids and

Your best friend

If you could only imagine

I'll love it forever and ever

If only I was your man

        If I Was Your Man

Incomplete

My life is incomplete without you

We were once one and now we're not

It's hard to live without you

I think a lot about you

I'm living an amazing life but it's

Incomplete without you

You were that main man in

My life

I'm now lost and hurt

I want my life back and complete

It's very sad

You've been on my mind the whole time

Unique Love: Quinton Simpson

And things doesn't feel right

Baby I'm tired of living this incomplete life

Come back and make it whole

Incomplete isn't what I was looking for in my life

I wanted a life of complete

My world was everything with you

If my world have to be incomplete

I don't want it because it doesn't mean

Me anything

I want something that's real, true and worth it

Let's be a team again

And be complete with each other

Incomplete isn't going to work

                      Incomplete

Just Friends

We're just friends and there's no need to fight

Over each other

When I tried to love you

You wouldn't let me nor would you

Let me care for you

I thought we were going to make something

Happen but you only wanted to be friends

And now since I'm in love

You want me in your life

I didn't think things would go this far

You were my best friend and now you

Want to be my main lover

It can happen because I'm in love

Unique Love: Quinton Simpson

You one had your chance

Friends you said we'll always be

I knew that wasn't going to happen

You always had crazy love for me

I can't see myself with you

We're friends and only friends

When I wanted to make you my girl

Your mind was playing games and my

Heart was being hurt

Through it all I'm good because you

Said we're just friends

                    Just Friends

Let It Go

I'm going to let our relationship go

It doesn't mean me anything

It's lost, weak and very misunderstood

And I do not love it

I'm giving it up and letting everything go

You didn't try to make it work

I was trying to make the best out of it

You through it all away

My heart was broken and I wanted to kill you

Trust is what I gave you, love is what

I showed you and loyal is what I was

I'm now letting it all go

I couldn't make you happy

Unique Love: Quinton Simpson

The more you faded away

You push me into letting this love go

My heart was always in the palm of

Your hands

Whatever you ask me to do

I did it

I thought you was the love of my life

But I see you wasn't

Our relationship was like a rock and

A hard place

I gave you the best love ever

My soul can't understand why you

Let everything go

I wanted you, loved you and you

Were my joy

Unique Love: Quinton Simpson

I hate to let go of something that once

Meant the world to me

And since you didn't care about us, our love

Nor our heart

I had to let you go

      Let It Go

Let Me Love You

Girl let me love you

You mean so much

You're the air I breathe

And the love I my heart

Baby I really love you

Unique Love: Quinton Simpson

Let me love your heart

Mind and soul

I'll take care of you

Baby I just want to enjoy you

Without you in my life

Things would be so different

Please let me love you

Without you in my life

Thiers no me

And I can't let that happen

You're my peace of mind

Let me take your heart, life and soul

Down that isle and make it official

Baby let me love and care for you

        Let Me Love You

Unique Love: Quinton Simpson

I Can't Stop Thinking About You

I can't stop thinking about our first kiss

It was genuine and amazing

The touch of your lips was lovely

My mind was in another world

You made me feel whole

I can't stop thinking about you

Because our love was like no other

You treated me with the upmost respect

I remember the time we had sex

It was a wow moment

Unique Love: Quinton Simpson

You put your all and more into it

Having my body feeling wonderful

The way you held my body had me

In another zone

Baby I loved it all

I can't seem to stop thinking about you

Your life brought kindness to my soul

Your heart is what I love the most

I can't stop thinking about the good times

We shared

They were real and heart felt

You was always the love of my life

Turned my life into an open book

And encourage me when I couldn't

Encourage myself

Unique Love: Quinton Simpson

This is why I can't stop thinking about

Someone like you

I Can't Stop Thinking About You

I should've known

I knew you didn't love me

You lied to me, wrecked my world

And even beat me

You was the love of my life, the joy in my heart

And the peace within my soul.

You treated me like dirt

Called me crazy names

And always lied to me

Unique Love: Quinton Simpson

I always love and cared for you

I was your whatever and didn't mean anything to you

I only strive to be the best

I was your number one fan

But you didn't love me.

When things got though you left

When life almost had me

And tried to kill me

You ran.

I should've known

If You Leave

If you leave my life

My world and heart

Would be lost

I can't focus without you

You're my flower that

Bloom in the spring time

Life will not be the same if you

Leave.

You're that rock in my soul

And the love in my mind

Baby please don't leave

You're my everything and more

Unique Love: Quinton Simpson

Leaving me is like leaving love

You'll break my world

You're my next and I'm your chapter

And if you leave me

Our hearts would be a close book

So baby please don't leave

        If You Leave

Unique Love: Quinton Simpson

Let's Wait a While

I would love to get to know you but I

Think we need to take things slow

You're a very nice person

We've always talked about getting together

The two of us have a lot in common

I really care about you

Let's wait a while and work on

Getting us together

I think we need to wait on the marriage

Thing because we still have a lot to learn

I'm not in a rush for it to happen

When the time come for us to make it happen

We'll be two happy people

Unique Love: Quinton Simpson

So let's wait a while and everything will fall in

Place

Waiting can be the best thing for us

It will teach us how to love more, stay

Humble and how to trust each other

Let's wait before we go half on a baby

That's something you really have to

Be ready for

And I think we can wait on that

So let's wait before we make anything happen

                    Let's Wait A While

Let My Lips

Let my lips feel your love

I want to feel the softness of your skin

And the moist of your body

My lips is ready for some good loving

There soft, amazing and ready to be use

I'm in the pleasing moment

My lips were made to lick on

You from head to toe

Their powerful, one of a kind

And very sweet

Unique Love: Quinton Simpson

You're forget the feeling

These lips will make you lose control

Let my lips play with your lips

Their hungry for a kiss, love

And some deep down licking

Let my sexy lips please and love you

Let My Lips

Life Without You

I can't imagine life without you

By my side

This is real love

Unique Love: Quinton Simpson

I'm feeling and I hope you feel the same way

Baby you mean so much to me

You bring out the best in me

Without in my amazing life

I'll feel lost and very unhappy

I can't see spending the rest

Of my life without you

You're the rock that keep me strong

And the love that keep me going

You're my everything

Life without you is worthless

Sad and lonely

I can't see myself without you

        Life Without You

Unique Love: Quinton Simpson

Love I'm yours

Love I belong to you

You mean the world

To me and I'm ready

To love again

Don't push me out of your life

We are meant to be together

Why run from me

I'm willing to let you in

I've missed you, I'm lonely

And I need you back

You were my back and I

Unique Love: Quinton Simpson

Were your bone

Love I'm all of yours

I need you, can't make it

Without you and can't seem

To think

Love you're my best friend, number

One fan and the believe in my life

Love I'm yours and more

So please come back because

I need you

                    Love I'm Yours

Unique Love: Quinton Simpson

Love You Down

Let me love you down

I don't care if it takes all night

I want to feel every inch of your body

Let me start at your lips

And work my way down to your funny part

Licking you like know other

Making your body feel priceless

Amazing and lovely

Let me love every part of you down with my love

Unique Love: Quinton Simpson

Can I love you down?

If it's for only one night

Love You Down

Lose My Mind

I'm about to lose my mind

I can't live my life without

My heart need you back

And my soul loves you

Come back baby because I need

You

I can't take this any longer

I'm about to lose my last mind

Unique Love: Quinton Simpson

I'm willing to lose my mind

If I can't spend the rest of my

Life with you

You're my everything and more

So please come back because my

Mind is lost, torn and don't understand

Help my mind before I lose it all

I can't think straight nor talk without

Thinking about you

My mind wants you back

I can't lose my mind but I'll

Do it for you

You mean the world to me

                Lose My Mind

Love You More

I love you more than life

You're my proud and joy

When life knock me down

You were there to pick me up

And this is why I love you more

Than ever

I'll always love you more than the rest

Because I know I have the best

You taught me about life and

How to be strong in those streets

You've given me love and more

This is why I love you more than ever

Unique Love: Quinton Simpson

The more I love you

The stronger my soul, body

And heart gets

I can't help how I feel about you

Words can't express how I feel about you

You help me when others gave up

On me and I would like to thank you

When life said no you can't

You pulled me by the ears and

Said yes you can.

And this is why I love you more

                Love You More

Unique Love: Quinton Simpson

Missing You

My heart is missing you like crazy

It hurt, torn and need you

It's hard to think about us

And I wish you come back

I really miss you

I was always treated like a king

That's what brought joy to my life

Baby I'm missing you like crazy

I can't take this anymore

The more my souls sleep

The more I begin to miss you

The late nights, early mornings

And amazing breakfast is what

Unique Love: Quinton Simpson

Missed the most

You was that family man

If I can only have you back

You took me on trips, bought me

Lavish things and gave me the world

I didn't have to want for anything

You put that happiness back in my life

I'm missing you like crazy

You were my other half and I

Need you back?

Missing someone isn't a good feeling

This is why I want you to come back

I miss you baby and will you please

Come back

                Missing You

Unique Love: Quinton Simpson

Must Be Nice

It must be nice to have a wonderful

Lady like you in his life

You're his everything

I can't go a day without hearing

Your voice

You're the woman that make his

Night go by

He's in love with you and it

Must be nice

You bring out the best in him

And he's your ride or die

The way he talk about you

Unique Love: Quinton Simpson

Bring joy to my life, peace

To my heart and love all over me

You two are so amazing and in love

You're his world that's always shining

Throughout the night, his moon that

Glow and his star that shine bright

He's crazy about you

It must be nice to have a wonderful

Man in your life

One who's loving, respectful and kind?

That man love you so much and I think

It's a lovely thing

He's your shield of protection and

He love you more than life

It must be nice to have a man like you

Nobody Knows

Nobody know how much I love you

You're my sweet heart, soul mate

And the queen of my night

I love you through your good, bad

And ugly

Nobody know how strong my love is for you

I'll go the extra mile, take risk after risk

And will put my life on the line for you

Nobody know the tears you cry at night

The pain you go through nor the broken heart

You once had

Unique Love: Quinton Simpson

I helped glued your life back together

Made you feel loved again

And feel like a real woman

I gave you my trust, heart and mind

Nobody know the love we shared nor

The things we've been through

Nobody Knows

Nothing in This World

It's nothing in this world that I wouldn't do for you

You're my backbone, you understand me and I'll

Always love you

Unique Love: Quinton Simpson

I'll go beyond whatever it takes

In order to keep you happy

Baby I really love you

Words really can't express the things that

I'll do for you

You've always been the love of my life

Life wasn't peaches and cream for me

Which I'm happy about because you

Came into my life and taught me a lot

You mixed my world back together

There's nothing in this world that

I wouldn't do for you

You gave me love when others hated me

Always told me to believe in myself and

Live life to the fullest

Unique Love: Quinton Simpson

This is why I'll go the extra mile for you

When life laughed in my face

You was the one who put me back together

And I thank you so much

It's nothing in this world that I wouldn't

Do for you

You're my proud and joy and

I'll always love you

                  Nothing In This World

Unique Love: Quinton Simpson

Part III

Unique Love: Quinton Simpson

Not My Type

I can't mess with your type

You sleep with anything that

Have legs, suck on anything that

Has lips and lay down with who ever

Baby girl you're not my type

I feel sorry for dead beats like you

Respect I'll never had for you

Because you mean nothing to me

I'm looking for a wife and not a whore

You're sad and I'll never see you as a lady

Women like you isn't for men nor my life

Walking around half naked, drunk and

Unique Love: Quinton Simpson

Looking like a rat isn't good

Nobody doesn't won't a nothing like you

You were made for men of steel because

You smell weird

I'll never date a girl like you

You'll sleep with my dog if I

Let you and that's sad

Grow up and get your life

You'll never be for me

I don't feel sorry for you because

A rat and a dummy you'll always be

You're a pretty girl but I just can't deal

With anyone like you

                Not My Type

Unique Love: Quinton Simpson

Say Yes

All you have to do is say yes

Open up your heart and let me

Love you

I won't to be your husband

Let's make this thing happen

You mean more than life to me

I want to make you mine

Baby so please says yes

I'm tired of being you boyfriend

It's about time I be your husband

Open up your heart and say yes

I'm in this for the long haul

I can't see myself without anyone

Unique Love: Quinton Simpson

But you

You're my love and joy

So baby come on and make this

Thing happen

If you say yes to me

I'll be the happiest man alive

You're my rock, my heart, the

Root of my soul and the better in me

I love, cherish and adore you

You make me feel whole, loved and

Amazing

Say yes and you'll make me the happiest

Man on earth

                Say Yes

Unique Love: Quinton Simpson

She Is

She's my world, love and my wife

She's the sun inn my sky, the moon

In the night and the stars all over

She's my everything and more.

She's the love in my voice, the peace in my soul

And the smile on my face.

She's the thought in my mind,

The movement of my fingers

And the curl of my toes

She'll always be my everything.

Unique Love: Quinton Simpson

She's my strength, power, love

And my number one girl.

She Is

So Sick

I'm so sick of love

It have treated me like nothing

And I very much hate it

I'm so sick of the way love once had me

I thought it was real

Until I woke up

And realize it was all a lie

Love can go to hell and back

Unique Love: Quinton Simpson

I'm not trying to be with it

Love doesn't love anyone

And I'm so sick of it

I gave love all of me

And still treated me as

If I was nothing

And I'm so sick of it

Love can go somewhere

And die because I'm tired of it

I've had enough of love

        So Sick

Unique Love: Quinton Simpson

Spending My Life With You

Spending my life with you is a living hell

You took me through it all

I was good to you, treated you with the

Upmost respect and always called you

My queen

I thought you were for me

The things you took me through

Were crazy and unkind

I really loved you

When life treated you like

Nothing

I was there to make things

Unique Love: Quinton Simpson

Better

You'll never find another man like me

I put everything I had in you

How could you still treat me like?

Nothing

Baby my feelings are done and out

I feel like nothing, love doesn't love

Me and I was just your whatever

I'll never spend my life with you again

                Spending My Life With You

Stick With You

I'm always going to stick with you

You're my baby and the beat of my heart

Nobody can't make me feel this way but

You

When our relationship went through the

Bad and the worse

You stuck it out

And this is why I love you

You're the mother of my child

My strength and the wow in my soul

You're the fire to my stomach, the

Wind of my pain and the eyes of my mind

You're my soul mate

Unique Love: Quinton Simpson

I love you so much and I must stick

With a good lady like you

I'm your left and you're my right

When life failed me, you never left

And I'm going to stick with you

I can't let you go out of my life

You're that shoulder to lean on

That heart to love and that smile on my face

Baby I love you and I'll always stick with you

        Stick With You

The Point Of It All

The point of it all loves you

We might fuss and fight about

Nothing but through it all I really

Love you

You mean the world to me and theirs

No leaving you or your heart

We're going to work out our bad

And love our good

The point of this is to show you how

Much I really love you

You're my baby and I'm your man

Unique Love: Quinton Simpson

The world would be lost without you

Not having you around would be worthless

You mean a lot to my life

And the point of it all is to love and

Care for you

You're a lovely lady, a wonderful mother

And a very important person

Your heart is filled with the most loving

Joy I know of

You filled my broken heart and put it

Back together

I was down and out but you once made me whole

The point of us is to one day become

Husband and wife, have a family and

Live life happy

Unique Love: Quinton Simpson

This is the point of me wanting to be

With a person like you

The Point Of It All

They Don't Know

The world don't know how

Much I love you

You're my strength, joy

And the love of my life

You're the push in my life

That positive thinking in

My mind and the love

On my face

Unique Love: Quinton Simpson

You're my support system

My main lady and the you

Can do it in my life

They don't know how much

I love you

We keep our love heart

And soul to each other

So there for they don't know

About our love

              They Don't Know

Unique Love: Quinton Simpson

Thinking Of You

Baby I been thinking of you

Your body keeps me warm, your lips

Keep me in love and your love keep

Me ready

I'm always thinking of you

Thinking of you bring me joy

Peace and happiness

Whenever you're not around

You're always on my mind

And I love you

Whenever thinking of you it brings

Unique Love: Quinton Simpson

Love and hope to my life

Whenever I'm down and out

I think of you because I know

Things will get better

You mean so much to my life

And I can't stop thinking of you

Thinking Of You

Tonight

Tonight I would love

To make love to you

Licking you from head to toe

Making your private part squeeze

Unique Love: Quinton Simpson

My lips and your eyes begin

To roll in the back of your head

Let me give you some of this good

Loving on tonight

I can't wait to taste and smell

That tight hole

My tongue is calling your body

On tonight

I would like to rub my fingers

Between your legs and

My lips across your body

Baby let me enjoy your body on tonight

I need some real loving

I'm willing to make your body feel

Amazing and priceless

Unique Love: Quinton Simpson

Come and give me some of

That great loving on tonight

Tonight

Torn

My life is torn between the two of you

I wanted to stay with you because of the love

You showed me or that's what I thought

Your life took me through hell and back

I was only good to you

People tried to tell me but I didn't listen

You gave me a dry penis to ride without

Any lube

Unique Love: Quinton Simpson

And I was that down freak in your life

I did whatever to keep you happy

Whenever you said jump I did

Only gave you the best and loved you

More than I loved myself

This is why I'm torn with you

I gave you my everything

You always showed me kindness

And kept it real

Life was amazing with you

True love is what they should

Call you

Your heart lived up to it

Respect should've been your

Nickname

Your soul showed it and more

Unique Love: Quinton Simpson

And this is one reason I'm torn

Between the two

Torn

Only If You Knew

Only if you knew how much

I loved you

You were once the love of

My life

You brought peace, happiness and

Joy in my life

You showed me respect, gave me

The world and always was there for me

Unique Love: Quinton Simpson

Only if you knew how much

My heart and soul missed you

You were my best friend and

The number one person in my

Life

You kept a smile on my face

Only if you knew how my world

Is without you

You was that better me

Things isn't the same

I miss you with everything I love

My miss your touch, love

And your smile

                Only If You Knew

Unique Love: Quinton Simpson

U Remind Me

U remind me of this

Girl I once loved

Every time I looked into her eyes

I remember all of the crazy things

She put me through

I thought she was the one for me

I should've known she was everybody

Girl

And I wanted her to be mine

U remind me of the way she dress

Looked and smile

I thought she was going to be my girl

Unique Love: Quinton Simpson

But she wanted to sex all of the boys

I put my trust in her

Every time you open your mouth

And unfold your lips

I feel a pile of lies

U remind me of the heart break

Sleepless nights and the lonely hours

I would like to be with you but you remind me

Of that girl I once loved and cared for

She was once my best but you remind me too

Much of her

                U Remind Me

Walk Away

No matter how hard

I try to walk out of your life

I can't walk away

Baby you mean so much to me

I'm stressing and don't know what to do

I need you in my life

And I won't to make you my wife

You're my lady and only lady

Walking out of your life isn't happening

I'm in this for the best

I love you baby and you're my world

Unique Love: Quinton Simpson

When things seem crazy, silly and unhappy

You always make things better

And I love you for that

Baby let's make this happen

Because I refuse to walk away

      Walk Away

What Am I Gonna Do

What am I gonna do

Without you in my life

You're my sugar and I'm your plum

Baby I need you in my life

Unique Love: Quinton Simpson

I'll be lost without you

What am I gonna do without you

In my heart, soul and world

You've always been my ride

And I'm always going to be your die

Loving you is like loving my self

I can't smile, cry nor think with out

You I my life

You're my pride and I will always be your

Loving joy

Baby don't leave me because my life would be done

And if you ever leave my wonderful life

What am I gonna do

You put that glow in my eyes that yes in my life

And the peace in my soul

So without you in my amazing world

I'll be crazy, silly and lost

Baby what am I gonna do

What Am I Gonna Do

What If

What if I tell you?

I didn't care about

You nor wanted to

Be with you

How would your feelings be?

Would you want to hurt me or

Unique Love: Quinton Simpson

Would you keep it moving?

What if I told you?

Our baby isn't yours

And I'm in love with

Someone else

How would you feel?

I might be in love with

Someone else man

What if I told you our

Relationship was fake,

You didn't mean anything

To me nor did I care

About your feelings

What if I told you?

Unique Love: Quinton Simpson

The world is more

Important than you

I sex your sister and

I never loved you

How would you feel?

What If

Who's Been Loving You?

Baby who's been loving you

Because you have joy in you

Eyes and peace all over your

Face

Unique Love: Quinton Simpson

Someone has been loving you

I can see the glow throughout

Your life

Who's been loving your heart

I see the kindness in your soul

And the love in yourself

I see your life is changing for the best

And I'm happy for you

Your sense of humor has change

Your smile is all over the place and

I see your happiness

So tell me the truth because I really

Want to know who's been loving you

Your walk have become sexy

Unique Love: Quinton Simpson

Your talk is flawless and your

Life is amazing

Baby who's been really loving you

Who's Been loving you

Why Break My Heart

I gave you the world

Took care of you and

Made things happen

You were my joy, my eyes

When I couldn't see and my strength

I gave you years of my life

Unique Love: Quinton Simpson

I was that love in your heart

Why break my heart when I only

Tried to give you the world, my life

And my happiness

When others made you cry

I was there to wipe your tears

Hold you through the night

And kiss you with love

So why break my heart

When I only wanted to love

And care for you.

        Why Break My Heart

Unique Love: Quinton Simpson

Why Him

I gave you my life, loved you,

and even tried to work things out

He gave you a heart attack;

Almost killed you and tried to drain your world.

You was my pride, joy, and my world;

you was my everything .

You was only a sideline in his book;

he treated you like hell, stepped all over you;

and made your life a living wreck.

I always called you my baby,

I gave you the best of me and you was that push in my life.

He called u his little dog, you was only his sex partner;

Unique Love: Quinton Simpson

he only loved you because you gave him the world.

I loved you, needed you, and

wanted to spend the rest of my life with you.

He only liked you, not wanted you;

and wanted you to be his sideline for the rest of your life.

Why him

Why O Why

Why tell a person something, you don't really mean

I loved you , cared for you;

But it seem like you wasn't loving me back.

I gave you my love, heart, and trust.

Unique Love: Quinton Simpson

I would kill for you die for you and even
would lie for you.

I gave you my life, turned on my family
and worked two jobs to take care of you.
When others low-rated you, I back you; put my life
on the line and even tried to hurt them.

I made your life, gave you the world
Always was your number one and never
let anyone talk about you.

I gave you sex, put up with your lies,
Cheating, and low-rating me; I still stuck by your side
and you wasn't loving me back, because you were too busy
loving someone else like my brother, why o why.

Unique Love: Quinton Simpson

Worth It

My love is worth it

I'm the best you'll ever have

I'm that respectful guy your mother

Always told you about, that guy your

Grandmother prayed about and the guy

That needs to be in your life

My love will be worth it

I'm the guy that will go the extra mile for you

Let's take this thing further because it's going

To be worth it

I'm willing to stand back and wait it out

I want you to be happy

Unique Love: Quinton Simpson

Our love will be worth it because

I'm willing to take things slow, show

You much love and will put in one hundred

Percent of overtime

Baby I love you

Let me show you and I promise it's going to be worth it

Worth It

You Are

You are the love of my life

The star that standout among

The rest and the lady in my life

Unique Love: Quinton Simpson

You are my every thing

You are my baby, the winter that

Bring cold and the summer that warms

It all

You are the perfect girl and

You're truly made for me

You are the reason I love

And you're the best in the world

I can't help but cry because you are

My number one girl

You're the only woman I'll ever

 Love

You're the reason why I work hard

And come home every night

You are my world

Unique Love: Quinton Simpson

You Are

You Call It Love

Baby boy you call it love

But I call it lust

You only want a quick nut

And I want to make love

There's a difference

You want to show me off in public

That's not cool because that's lust

And not love

I see the lust all in your eyes

It's something about them that

Unique Love: Quinton Simpson

Make my skin crawl

The love isn't their but that's

What you call it

You always imagine sexing me in

Your mind

Which is lust or I could be wrong

In your eyes its only love

I'm lost for words because everything in your

World is love and only love

If you call it love

I call it whatever because that's

What it is

You showed me your life live on lust

But you call it love

Unique Love: Quinton Simpson

You Call It Love

You Mean The World To Me

You mean so much to me

You're my everything

Anything I can do for you let me know

You're the blue in my shy, the crave in my mouth

And the power of my heart

You're my more and more

You're awesome to me, amazing and loyal

That's why you mean the world to me

Unique Love: Quinton Simpson

You're that tie of my heart, that lick of my tongue

And that shine on my teeth

Baby you're my world and all

You mean the world to me

You Mean The World To Me

You

I love you baby

You're the root of

My heart, the soul of

My life and the water that

Run through my soul

Unique Love: Quinton Simpson

I love the way you

Move my life, sleep

In my arms throughout the night

And the way you love me

I always wanted to be with you

You put that love, trust

And kindness back in my heart

You're my only girl

You keep me humble, filled with love

And keep it sexy

Without you in my life where would I be?

You're my proud and I'm your amazing

And loving joy

                    You

Unique Love: Quinton Simpson

Unique Love: Quinton Simpson

www.ingramcontent.com/pod-product-compliance
Lightning Source LLC
Chambersburg PA
CBHW071438160426
43195CB00013B/1956